W9-BFK-877

Anaheim Ducks

Nick Day

AV² provides enriched content that supplements and complements this book. Weigl's AV² books strive to create inspired learning and engage young minds in a total learning experience.

Your AV² Media Enhanced books come alive with...

Audio
Listen to sections of the book read aloud.

Key Words
Study vocabulary, and complete a matching word activity.

Video
Watch informative video clips.

Quizzes
Test your knowledge.

Go to www.av2books.com, and enter this book's unique code.

BOOK CODE

G 9 2 6 4 7 3

Embedded Weblinks
Gain additional information for research.

Slide Show
View images and captions, and prepare a presentation.

AV² by Weigl brings you media enhanced books that support active learning.

Try This!
Complete activities and hands-on experiments.

... and much, much more!

Published by AV² by Weigl
350 5th Avenue, 59th Floor
New York, NY 10118
Websites: www.av2books.com   www.weigl.com

Library of Congress Control Number: 2014951925

ISBN 978-1-4896-3110-7 (hardcover)
ISBN 978-1-4896-3111-4 (single-user eBook)
ISBN 978-1-4896-3112-1 (multi-user eBook)

Printed in the United States of America in Brainerd, Minnesota
1 2 3 4 5 6 7 8 9 0   19 18 17 16 15

032015
WEP050315

Senior Editor Heather Kissock
Art Director Terry Paulhus

Photo Credits
Every reasonable effort has been made to trace ownership and to obtain permission to reprint copyright material. The publishers would be pleased to have any errors or omissions brought to their attention so that they may be corrected in subsequent printings.

Weigl acknowledges Getty Images and iStock as its primary image suppliers for this title.

Anaheim Ducks

CONTENTS

AV² Book Code. 2
Introduction 4
History .6
The Arena. 8
Where They Play 10
The Uniforms 12
Helmets and Face Masks 14
The Coaches 16
Fans and the Internet. 18
Legends of the Past 20
Stars of Today. 22
All-Time Records 24
Timeline 26
Write a Biography 28
Trivia Time 30
Key Words/Index 31
www.av2books.com. 32

Introduction

The Anaheim Ducks are a fairly young **franchise**, but after just 21 seasons in the National Hockey League (NHL), they have compiled a colorful and dramatic history. They are the only team in the history of American sports that was inspired by a fictional movie, *The Mighty Ducks,* in 1992. Thanks to the players' unique talents, the team has made a name for itself beyond the Disney film that led to its creation. In 2007, the team won its first and only Stanley Cup.

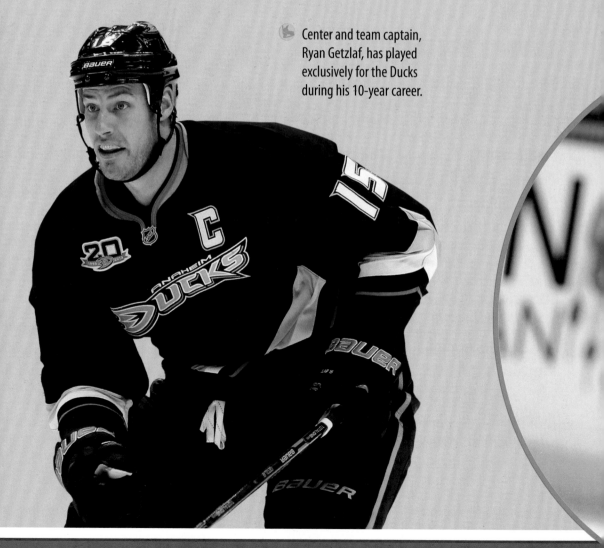

Center and team captain, Ryan Getzlaf, has played exclusively for the Ducks during his 10-year career.

The Ducks are one of two NHL teams in sunny southern California, which has not historically been a hockey hot-spot. The Los Angeles Kings had begun play several years earlier, introducing southern Californians to hockey. The Ducks are now the Kings' closest rivals, and continue on their path to another Stanley Cup victory.

Anaheim DUCKS

The Ducks have played in two Stanley Cup Finals in their 21-year history. Stefan Noesen and other young stars hope to add another Cup in the near future.

Arena Honda Center

Division Pacific

Head Coach Bruce Boudreau

Location Anaheim, California

NHL Stanley Cup Titles 2007

Nicknames The Mighty Ducks

1
Stanley Cup

10
Playoff Appearances

3
Division Titles

10
Playoff-series Victories

History

1 Only one Ducks player has ever had his number retired.

Paul Kariya played nine seasons in Anaheim. In four of those seasons, the left wing played all 82 games.

In December 1992, the Walt Disney Company announced it would purchase an **expansion** hockey franchise and the team would play in Orange County, California. Earlier that year, Disney had produced *The Mighty Ducks*, a film about a children's hockey team. Disney's new real-life hockey team would be called the Mighty Ducks of Anaheim, playing just down the road from Disneyland.

As with any new team, it took the Mighty Ducks a few seasons to find their footing. They first made the **playoffs** in the 1996–1997 season, but only advanced through one round. The Ducks started to see real success in the 2002–2003 season. With the addition of a group of talented players from around the NHL, the team came together under the leadership of coach Mike Babcock, reaching the Stanley Cup Finals in 2003. Though they came up empty that season, the Ducks won the Stanley Cup in 2007.

In the 2006 season, the Mighty Ducks were bought by the Samueli family, which renamed the team the "Anaheim Ducks." With plenty of young, offensive firepower, the Ducks have become a force in the Pacific Division and beyond.

As Disney Chief Executive Officer, Eisner was instrumental in establishing the Mighty Ducks of Anaheim.

The Arena

The Honda Center, which was first called Arrowhead Pond, has been the home of the Ducks since their very first game in 1993.

The Honda Center was completed in 1993, but at the time of its opening, the state-of-the-art arena was called the Arrowhead Pond. In 2006, Honda assumed the title **sponsorship** from Arrowhead, and the building was renamed.

Honda Center, also known as The Pond or The Ponda, hosts sold-out concerts and special events when the Ducks are not skating. In fact, the well-respected arena was recently voted as one of the world's top ten arenas by *Venues Today* magazine. Fans and critics love Honda Center for its sleek design and intimate setting. Even though there are about 17,000 seats, everyone feels close to the action, as the distance from the highest seat to the ice is only 82 feet (25 meters).

Ducks fans love the luxury clubs and suites at the Honda Center. The Grand Terrace, which was added in October 2013, is a beautiful indoor/outdoor entertainment space with more than 100 feet (30.5 m) of concession area. The Grand Terrace is a traditional California-style space, complete with palm trees, sunshine, and cool breezes, all in a setting of luxury.

"The Pond" is not only a hockey arena. It also hosts concerts featuring popular stars like Jennifer Lopez. Although Honda Center only holds about 17,000 seats, the entire arena can hold nearly 19,000 concert-goers at its sold-out shows.

Where They Play

CANADA

British Columbia **7**

Alberta **4**

3

Saskatchewan

Manitoba **14**

Ontario

Washington

Montana

North Dakota

Minnesota **11**

Wisconsin

8

Oregon

Idaho

South Dakota

UNITED

Iowa

Illinois

6

Nevada

Wyoming

Nebraska

STATES

13

Missouri

California

Utah

Colorado **9**

Kansas

5

1

Honda Center, Anaheim

Arizona **2**

New Mexico

Oklahoma

Arkansas

Mississ

Pacific Ocean

MEXICO

Texas **10**

Louisiana

Gulf of Mexico

NHL WESTERN CONFERENCE

PACIFIC DIVISION

★ 1   Anaheim Ducks
2   Arizona Coyotes
3   Calgary Flames
4   Edmonton Oilers

5   Los Angeles Kings
6   San Jose Sharks
7   Vancouver Canucks

CENTRAL DIVISION

8   Chicago Blackhawks
9   Colorado Avalanche
10   Dallas Stars
11   Minnesota Wild

12   Nashville Predators
13   St. Louis Blues
14   Winnipeg Jets

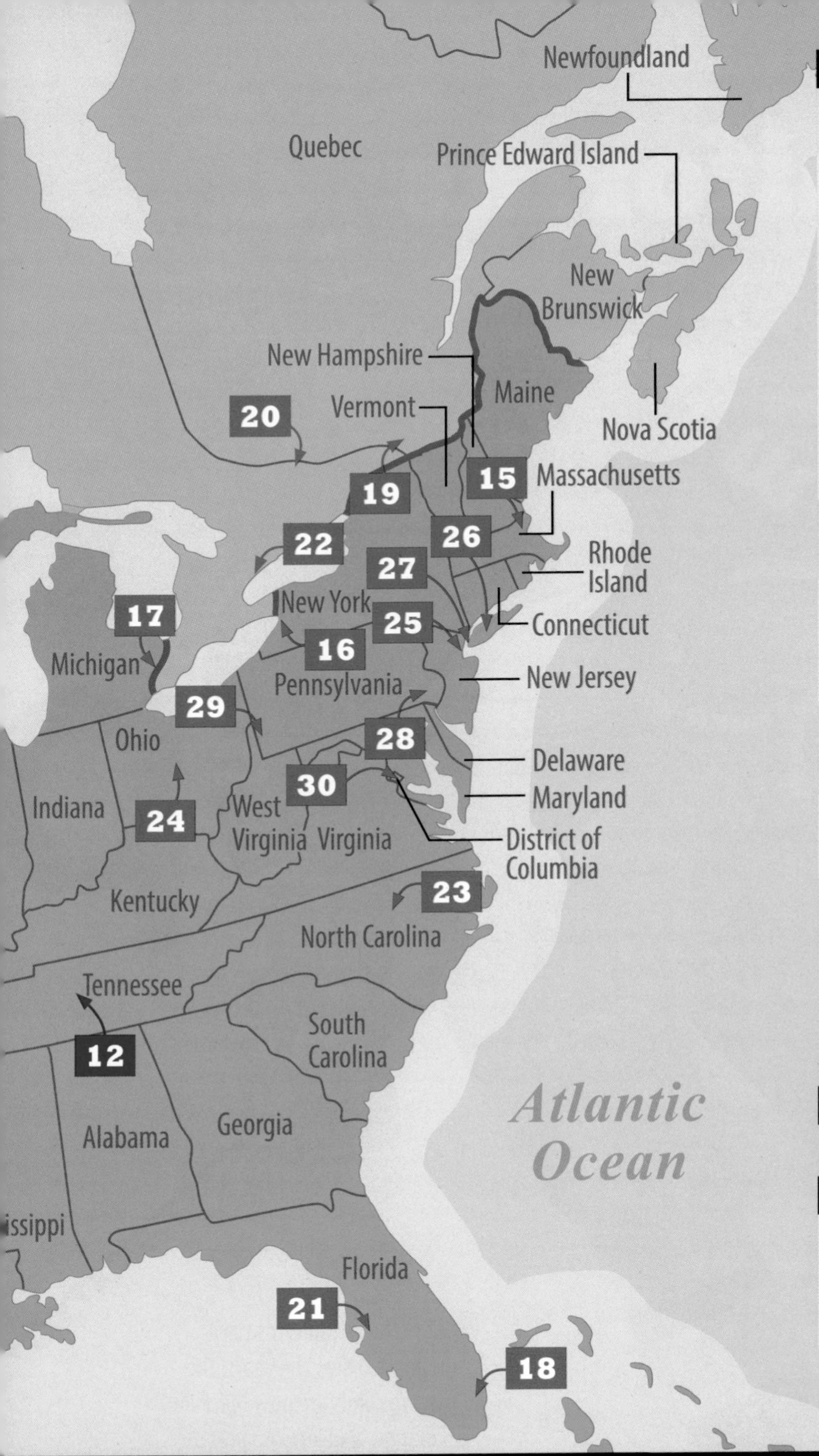
Newfoundland
Quebec
Prince Edward Island
New Brunswick
New Hampshire
Vermont
Maine
Nova Scotia
Massachusetts
Rhode Island
New York
Connecticut
Michigan
Pennsylvania
New Jersey
Ohio
Delaware
Maryland
Indiana
West Virginia
Virginia
District of Columbia
Kentucky
North Carolina
Tennessee
South Carolina
Alabama
Georgia
issippi
Florida
Atlantic Ocean
20
19
15
22
26
27
17
25
16
29
28
30
24
23
12
21
18

HONDA Center

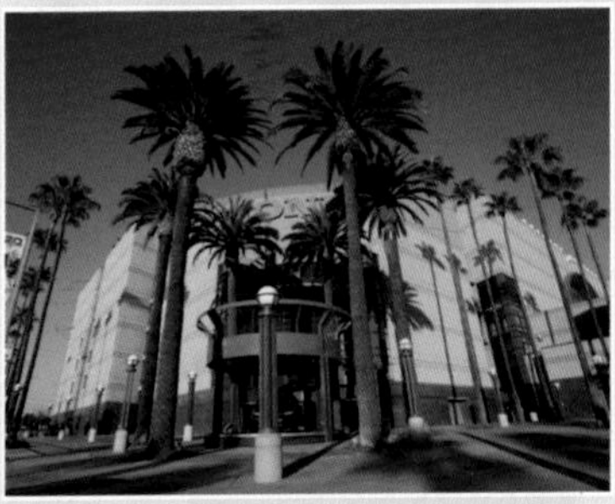

Arena
Honda Center

Location
2695 East Katella Avenue
Anaheim, CA 92806

Broke Ground
November 8, 1990

Completed
June 19, 1993

Features
- 83 luxury suites
- 500 HDTVs
- more than 130 palm trees
- more than 200,000 square feet (18,581 square meters) of marble

LEGEND
- ☆ Honda Center
- Eastern Conference
- Western Conference

ATLANTIC DIVISION

15 Boston Bruins
16 Buffalo Sabres
17 Detroit Red Wings
18 Florida Panthers
19 Montreal Canadiens
20 Ottawa Senators
21 Tampa Bay Lightning
22 Toronto Maple Leafs

METROPOLITAN DIVISION

23 Carolina Hurricanes
24 Columbus Blue Jackets
25 New Jersey Devils
26 New York Islanders
27 New York Rangers
28 Philadelphia Flyers
29 Pittsburgh Penguins
30 Washington Capitals

The Uniforms

10

The Ducks have made 10 separate uniform changes.

The Ducks' uniforms have changed over the years. The team colors are now black and orange, and jerseys sport a gold letter "D" that is shaped like a duck's webbed foot.

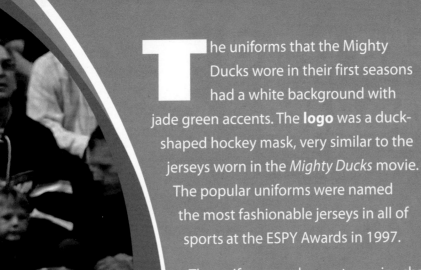

The uniforms that the Mighty Ducks wore in their first seasons had a white background with jade green accents. The **logo** was a duck-shaped hockey mask, very similar to the jerseys worn in the *Mighty Ducks* movie. The popular uniforms were named the most fashionable jerseys in all of sports at the ESPY Awards in 1997.

HOME

The uniforms underwent a major change in 2006. In an effort to rebrand the team as a more serious hockey organization, the Samueli family designed a new logo and a color scheme, adding a black background with gold lettering. They also added in subtle orange accents to further connect the color to the team's home, Orange County.

AWAY

The color orange was introduced on Ducks' jerseys subtly in 2006. Over the years, though, the color has begun to appear more boldly.

Helmets and Face Masks

In the old days of hockey, before the Ducks even existed, it was legal, and common, for players to **NOT WEAR A HELMET.**

Today's high-tech helmets, combined with clear plastic visors, provide protection for players like Corey Perry, who move at high speeds and often collide with other players.

The Ducks' current helmets are black, to match their nearly all-black uniforms. The large Ducks logo is located on the sides of the helmets. The logo is the same large, duck-foot-shaped "D" which appears on the team's jerseys. The "D" is gold, underlined in orange, and designed to look like it is moving fast, like a speeding hockey player. The gold "D" replaced the prior logo, which was the entire word "Ducks" written in gold lettering.

The Ducks have a tradition of bold face masks. The high praise the original Mighty Ducks logo received from players and fans inspired Anaheim's goalies to be creative in customizing their own helmets. Most of the Ducks' goalie helmets have featured fierce cartoon duck faces. The base of the mask near the chin is usually orange or gold, the mask itself white, and all of the design elements are flashy, fun, and often personal.

Ducks goalie John Gibson is famous for his creative helmets, including the self-designed and popular Pac-man themed mask.

The Coaches

1 Randy Carlyle brought Anaheim its only Stanley Cup, and coached the team for seven seasons.

Hoisting the Stanley Cup over his head is not as easy as Coach Carlyle made it look. The trophy is 35.25 inches (33.66 centimeters) long and weighs 34.5 pounds (15.6 kilograms).

The Ducks have had a total of eight coaches in team history. In searching for a winning formula, the organization moved through coaches quickly, with an average tenure of less than three years. However, after their 2007 Stanley Cup victory, their coaching carousel has begun to stabilize.

MIKE BABCOCK Mike Babcock made an immediate impact as the Ducks head coach, directing them to their best season in franchise history in 2003. Babcock oversaw the team's run to the Stanley Cup Finals, where they were defeated by the New Jersey Devils. Although this was a difficult loss, it cemented the young Ducks as a competitive NHL franchise.

RANDY CARLYLE Randy Carlyle enjoyed immediate success as the head coach of the Anaheim Ducks. In his first season behind the bench, he led his team to 43 regular season wins and an appearance in the Conference Final. Carlyle then took his team two steps further the following season by not only reaching the Stanley Cup Final, but winning it as well. Though Carlyle left the franchise during the 2011–2012 season, the Ducks enjoyed a great run under his leadership, reaching the playoffs in five of his six full seasons.

BRUCE BOUDREAU Bruce Boudreau was hired in 2011–2012 after the team got off to a horrible 6–20 win/loss start. In his first two years at the helm of the Ducks, Boudreau has compiled a solid regular season record. With only one playoff series victory, he now needs to prove himself as a capable postseason coach in Anaheim.

Fans and the Internet

By day, Ducks fans can visit nearby Disneyland before enjoying an NHL game at The Pond, which is just a few miles (kilometers) away from the theme park.

A Ducks fan tradition is to celebrate the colors of the team. Many fans do this by painting their faces, using both black and orange, the team's main colors. They also wear big and bold orange wigs. During playoff games, the organization gives out orange rally towels, which fans wave over their heads. After a Ducks goal, the stands become a swirling sea of orange. In addition, Ducks fans sing a special song after each goal, "Bro Hymn" by local southern California band, Pennywise.

The Ducks' official website has a chat room for fans to discuss their team. There is always a sense of excitement in Anaheim about the Ducks, and fans love going online to share it with one another. For fans interested in learning more about the Ducks, AnaheimCalling is a blog that offers a forum to discuss and debate all things Ducks.

Signs
of a fan

#1 Ducks fans are known to wear team jerseys, wave towels, and celebrate especially loudly at home games.

#2 The half-orange, half-black, face paint is a classic die-hard Ducks fan tradition.

Legends of the Past

Many great players have suited up for the Ducks. A few of them have become icons of the team and the city it represents.

Paul Kariya

Paul Kariya was drafted in the first round of the 1993 NHL Entry Draft. He began playing for the Ducks in the following season, and was immediately seen as one of the team's most successful and important players. The fans also had a soft spot for Kariya because he was with the Ducks almost from the beginning of the team's history. Kariya's best season with the Ducks was 1995–1996, during which he scored 50 goals. Kariya led the team in goals scored in five of his nine seasons in Anaheim. Kariya left the team in 2003.

Position: Left Wing
NHL Seasons: 15 (1994–2010)
Born: October 16, 1974,
in Vancouver, British Columbia, Canada

Teemu Selanne

Teemu Selanne was drafted in the first round of the 1988 NHL **Entry Draft** by the Winnipeg Jets and began playing for the Ducks in the 1995 season. He played 15 NHL seasons with the Ducks, during which he led the team in goals scored five times. Selanne holds the team record of 52 goals in a single season, during 1997–1998. Selanne has led the Ducks to two Stanley Cup Final appearances, including one victory. Selanne retired at the end of the 2013–2014 season, and his number 8 jersey was retired.

Position: Right Wing
NHL Seasons: 15 (1995–2001, 2005–2014)
Born: July 3, 1970, in Helsinki, Finland

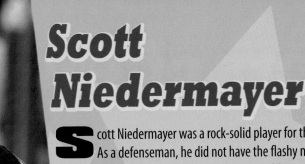

Scott Niedermayer

Scott Niedermayer was a rock-solid player for the Ducks. As a defenseman, he did not have the flashy numbers of offensive teammates such as Paul Kariya and Teemu Selanne. Niedermayer was known for his toughness and durability. In fact, during the 2008–2009 season, he played all 82 games. He was the highest-scoring defenseman on the team for four seasons, and in the 2006–2007 season, he scored 69 points, the most ever by a Ducks defenseman. Niedermayer was a fan favorite. He was a low-key player who rarely got into fights or showed much emotion, but he was a reliable player who led by example.

Position: Defenseman
NHL Seasons: 18 (1991–2010)
Born: August 31, 1973, in Edmonton, Alberta, Canada

Steve Rucchin

Steve Rucchin established himself as one of the Ducks' most dependable players during his time in Anaheim. Rucchin was a gifted playmaker who always seemed to be in the middle of scoring plays. In the 1997–1998 season, he led the team with 36 **assists**. Although Rucchin left the Ducks before their first Stanley Cup Championship in 2007, he played a central role in Anaheim's rise from expansion team to Stanley Cup champions.

Position: Center
NHL Seasons: 12 (1994–2007)
Born: July 4, 1971, in Thunder Bay, Ontario, Canada

Stars of Today

oday's Ducks team is made up of many young, talented players who have proven that they are among the best in the league.

Ryan Getzlaf

yan Getzlaf is in his fourth season as the Ducks' captain, and his ninth with the team. Getzlaf is the team's emotional leader and perhaps its best playmaker as well. The 2013–2014 season was one of his best, as Getzlaf was second in the NHL in total points, with 87, for the year. That same season, he led Anaheim in both scoring and assists. In 2014, Getzlaf also set a team record for career postseason points, with 74. The Ducks recently signed Getzlaf through the 2020 season, so he can be at the center of their championship dreams for years to come.

Position: Center
NHL Seasons: 9 (2005–Present)
Born: May 10, 1985, in Regina, Saskatchewan, Canada

Corey Perry

orey Perry is one of the NHL's many unsung heroes. Although he has brought much excitement to Anaheim with his unique offensive skill set, he rarely gets the accolades. In the 2013–2014 season, Perry led the NHL in even-strength goals with 35, and finished second in goals overall. He netted a career-best 50 goals during the 2010–2011 season. He made Ducks history by surpassing Selanne for a team record 34 career playoff assists. Perry has excellent offensive instincts as well as a very solid frame.

Position: Right Wing
NHL Seasons: 9 (2005–Present)
Born: May 16, 1985, in Peterborough, Ontario, Canada

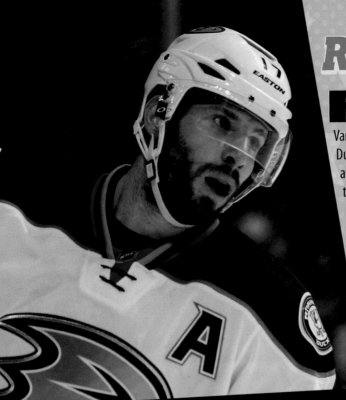

Ryan Kesler

Ryan Kesler was a new addition to the 2014–2015 Anaheim Ducks team, having been traded from the Vancouver Canucks at the end of the 2013–2014 season. During the majority of his time in Vancouver, Kesler scored at least 20 goals a year. In the 2010–2011 season, he put the puck in the net 41 times, a career and team high. Kesler is a fierce and durable competitor who can be counted on to appear in the lineup nightly. Now in his 11th season, Kesler has already had seven seasons in which he played 70 or more games.

Position: Center
NHL Seasons: 11 (2003–Present)
Born: August 31, 1984, in Livonia, Michigan, United States

Cam Fowler

Cam Fowler is one of Anaheim's most promising prospects. He has already been signed through the 2017 season. Fowler improved upon his already stellar numbers in 2013–2014, leading Anaheim defensemen in scoring, assists, and points per game. Fowler came to the NHL when he was just 18 years old, having graduated from Farmington High School in Michigan. He also won Gold at the 2010 World Junior Championship, a very high honor in youth hockey. The Ducks are hoping that Fowler is the NHL's next superstar—a player they can build around for many years to come.

Position: Defenseman
NHL Seasons: 4 (2010–Present)
Born: December 5, 1991, in Windsor, Ontario, Canada

All-Time Records

457
Career Goals
Teemu Selanne was an absolute scoring machine. In addition to this record, he holds many other Ducks offensive records that will not soon be surpassed.

66
Assists in a Season
Getzlaf is the ultimate teammate, spreading the puck around to give his teammates scoring opportunities.

54
Wins in a Season (2013–2014)

It is no surprise that this record was set in the same season as the team's goals record. The Ducks had it all figured out in 2013–2014 and advanced to the NHL Conference Semi-Finals.

263
Team Goals in a Single Season (2013–2014)

This was a great year for the Ducks. Everything clicked as they scored a record number of goals.

92.4
Highest Save Percentage in a Season

The Ducks do not have a storied history with goaltenders, but Jonas Hiller set an impressive record in the 2010–2011 season with this stunning **save percentage**.

Timeline

Throughout the team's history, the Anaheim Ducks have had many memorable events that have become defining moments for the team and its fans.

1992
The NHL announces that the Walt Disney Company has been awarded an expansion team. The new team is named the Mighty Ducks of Anaheim, after Disney's successful kids' movie.

1993
The Mighty Ducks announce that Ron Wilson will be the first head coach of the team. He was an assistant coach with the Vancouver Canucks. Wilson would coach three unimpressive seasons with the Ducks before being released.

| 1990 | 1992 | 1994 | 1996 | 1998 | 2000 |

The Mighty Ducks organization announces that the team will play at the Arrowhead Pond in Anaheim, a beautiful, brand new concert venue not far from Disneyland.

1998
Craig Hartsburg is hired as head coach with the hope of breathing some new life into a franchise that is still figuring out how to win consistently.

1995
Paul Kariya joins the Mighty Ducks, bringing new life to the franchise. Although the Mighty Ducks do not contend for the playoffs that season, they put themselves on a path to future success.

The Future
The Ducks have figured out how to win big games. While they have yet to make it back to the Stanley Cup Final, the Ducks have made the playoffs three times in the past four seasons. The team and the organization have work to do in order to add another championship banner to the rafters, but the Ducks have certainly come a long way in their short history.

2005
Henry and Susan Samueli buy the team from the Walt Disney Company for more than $50 million. The team is now permanently separated from Disney.

In 2007, the Ducks advance all the way to the Stanley Cup Final—and win. They defeat the Ottawa Senators in five games, capping off the most successful season in team history.

| 2002 | 2003 | 2006 | 2009 | 2012 | 2015 |

2003
The Mighty Ducks stun the defending champion Red Wings by sweeping them in the first round of the playoffs. They then advance to the Stanley Cup Final, where they lose to the Devils.

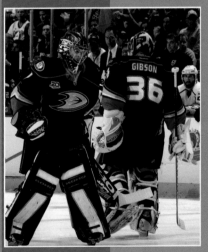

2014
The Ducks advance to the second round of the playoffs and face their crosstown rivals, the Los Angeles Kings. The seven-game series is tight and includes one overtime win, one tie, and three games with a single goal differential. Ultimately, the Kings advance.

Write a Biography

Life Story

A person's life story can be the subject of a book. This kind of book is called a biography. Biographies often describe the lives of people who have achieved great success. These people may be alive today, or they may have lived many years ago. Reading a biography can help you learn more about a great person.

Get the Facts

Use this book, and research in the library and on the internet, to find out more about your favorite Duck. Learn as much about him as you can. What position does he play? What are his statistics in important categories? Has he set any records? Also, be sure to write down key events in the person's life. What was his childhood like? What has he accomplished off the field? Is there anything else that makes this person special or unusual?

Use the Concept Web

A concept web is a useful research tool. Read the questions in the concept web on the following page. Answer the questions in your notebook. Your answers will help you write a biography.

Concept Web

Adulthood
- Where does this individual currently reside?
- Does he or she have a family?

Your Opinion
- What did you learn from the books you read in your research?
- Would you suggest these books to others?
- Was anything missing from these books?

Childhood
- Where and when was this person born?
- Describe his or her parents, siblings, and friends.
- Did this person grow up in unusual circumstances?

Accomplishments off the Field
- What is this person's life's work?
- Has he or she received awards or recognition for accomplishments?
- How have this person's accomplishments served others?

Write a Biography

Help and Obstacles
- Did this individual have a positive attitude?
- Did he or she receive help from others?
- Did this person have a mentor?
- Did this person face any hardships?
- If so, how were the hardships overcome?

Accomplishments on the Field
- What records does this person hold?
- What key games and plays have defined his career?
- What are his stats in categories important to his position?

Work and Preparation
- What was this person's education?
- What was his or her work experience?
- How does this person work?
- What is the process he or she uses?

Trivia Time

Take this quiz to test your knowledge of the Anaheim Ducks. The answers are printed upside down under each question.

1 What were the two names of the Ducks' arena?

A. Arrowhead Pond and Honda Center

2 How many times have the Ducks competed in the Stanley Cup Final?

A. Two

3 Which company was the first owner of the Mighty Ducks when they were created in 1993?

A. The Walt Disney Company

4 Which NHL team is the Ducks' crosstown rival?

A. The Los Angeles Kings

5 What division do the Ducks play in?

A. Pacific

6 How many coaches have the Ducks had during their existence?

A. Eight

7 Which Anaheim Duck holds the team record for most career goals?

A. Teemu Selanne

8 Who is the Ducks' 2014–2015 team captain?

A. Ryan Getzlaf

9 What is the Ducks' current logo?

A. A large gold "D" designed to look like a webbed foot

Key Words

assists: a statistic that is attributed to up to two players of the scoring team who shoot, pass, or deflect the puck toward the scoring teammate

entry draft: an annual meeting where different teams in the NHL are allowed to pick new, young players who can join their teams

expansion: expansion in the NHL is marked by the addition of a new franchise. The league last expanded in 2000 when the Columbus Blue Jackets and Minnesota Wild joined the NHL.

franchise: a team that is a member of a professional sports league

logo: a symbol that stands for a team or organization

playoffs: a series of games that occur after regular season play

save percentage: the rate at which a goalie stops shots being made toward his net by the opposing team

sponsorship: to support an NHL team financially in exchange for the promotion of a certain company's products or services

Index

Arrowhead Pond 8, 9, 26, 30

Babcock, Mike 7, 17
Boudreau, Bruce 5, 17

Carlyle, Randy 16, 17

Disney 4, 7, 26, 27, 30
Disneyland 18, 26

Fowler, Cam 23

Getzlaf, Ryan 4, 22, 24, 30

Hartsburg, Craig 26
helmet 14, 15
Hiller, Jonas 25
Honda Center 5, 8, 9, 10, 11, 30

Kariya, Paul 6, 20, 21, 26
Kesler, Ryan 23

logo 13, 15, 30, 31

movie 4, 13, 26

Niedermayer, Scott 21

Pacific Division 5, 7, 10
Perry, Corey 14, 22

Rucchin, Steve 21

Samueli family 7, 13, 27
Selanne, Teemu 20, 21, 22, 24, 30

uniform 12, 13, 15

Wilson, Ron 26

Log on to www.av2books.com

AV² by Weigl brings you media enhanced books that support active learning. Go to www.av2books.com, and enter the special code found on page 2 of this book. You will gain access to enriched and enhanced content that supplements and complements this book. Content includes video, audio, weblinks, quizzes, a slide show, and activities.

AV² Online Navigation

Audio
Listen to sections of the book read aloud.

Book Pages
AV² pages directly correspond to pages in the book.

Video
Watch informative video clips.

Key Words
Study vocabulary, and complete a matching word activity.

Embedded Weblinks
Gain additional information for research.

Quizzes
Test your knowledge.

Slide Show
View images and captions, and prepare a presentation.

Try This!
Complete activities and hands-on experiments.

AV² was built to bridge the gap between print and digital. We encourage you to tell us what you like and what you want to see in the future.

Sign up to be an AV² Ambassador at www.av2books.com/ambassador.

Due to the dynamic nature of the Internet, some of the URLs and activities provided as part of AV² by Weigl may have changed or ceased to exist. AV² by Weigl accepts no responsibility for any such changes. All media enhanced books are regularly monitored to update addresses and sites in a timely manner. Contact AV² by Weigl at 1-866-649-3445 or av2books@weigl.com with any questions, comments, or feedback.